love in the age of quarantine

poems

Katie Feltmate

Love in the Age of Quarantine Copyright © 2021 Katie Feltmate
All rights reserved. No part of this book may be used, sold or
copied without the author's explicit consent except for the use
of quotes and excerpts for the purpose of reviews and articles.

katiefeltmate.com

Illustrations by Kyla Porter
Cover Design by Nskvsky
ISBN: 978-1-7776097-0-2

content warning

parts of this book contain sensitive content around intimate partner abuse, loss, disordered eating, body image, grief, and mental illness. please practice self-care when reading.

forward from the author

it was a year of writing through grief, heartache, uncertainty, and pain. of writing when i was tired and writing when i was sick. of writing when i was happy and in love and writing when i was breaking. it was a year of writing my way back to myself.

it was an age when creating routine became survival and socializing became computer screens. an age when the whole world changed together, grieved together, fought together, and began to heal together. it was an age where human touch became lethal, and love meant distance. it was an age of learning how to love differently.

and here i am
standing on the other side of it all
the most fragile parts of me
beat in your hands now

contents

isolation 8

excavation 51

holding hands 94

linking arms 130

to write it down
the highest point of healing
to call it by name not just by feeling
to shine a spotlight on what you could not
bear to look at before
to stand face to face with your trauma
to study every pore
to spell it out in a fringe of phonetics
to see your truths lying naked on the page
to craft your pain into cursive aesthetics
to watch it dance on a coil-bound stage
to write it down
the highest point of healing
to write it down

dear reader   remember
no matter what season of change
our world undergoes when firm
ground becomes the crumble
of loose rock eroding
remember
to love
first

isolation

katie feltmate

the explosion will deafen your ears and leave you reeling
the shards of debris will cut open the bareness of your feet
and for a while everything will be red
everything will be ending and desperate and loud
your lungs will house the smoke
your eyes will try to vanquish the flames
finally, the ground will stop shaking
and the burning will cease
and when you are left with nothing
but ash in every direction
how easy it is to want to sweep it all up
and put it together again
but this is not the place
to rebuild

love in the age of quarantine

a man
who sees how brightly
you are shining
as a threat to his universe
will never stop trying to eclipse you

katie feltmate

you punched a hole in the wall
and i put a frame around the cracked plaster
and called it art
called it an accident
called it forgiven

love in the age of quarantine

the first woman to die during covid-19 in my province
died not from the virus
but from the hands of her husband
isolation, stress, a lethal combination in
a home stuffed with gunpowder insulation
it only takes the strike of one match
to set it off

i think about her fear
and it brings me back to mine
my apartment morphs back into crime scene
i can see the yellow tape draped across the door
i can hear the wince of my coffee table
maimed from being uprooted and thrown on its back
i can smell the burnt flesh of his charred tongue
still smoking on the ground

and all of a sudden it is december
covid-19 is not yet part of my vernacular
and i am sitting on the edge
of the bathtub
door locked
praying the bolts in the hinges
aren't as old as this house
i am shaking, my lungs collapsing
and expanding themselves in desperation
as if they are trying to build up enough momentum
to float up my throat
                and hang glide
                        off my
                              tongue

this is when i realize my lips
have been moving this whole time
chanting, self-soothing myself
like a mother to a child
i am okay
i am okay

i try to remember that i am okay
i am not there and it is not december
it's april and i am sitting at my dining room
table in the late hours of the night
attempting to write about her trauma
but ending up writing
about mine

and aren't they the same thing anyway

-for tracey mackenzie

love in the age of quarantine

to quarantine alone in a pandemic
when you are freshly cut up from a breakup
is a special kind of sting

        to quarantine alone in a pandemic
when you are freshly cut up from an abusive relationship
            is a whole other kind of ache

katie feltmate

i was self-isolating long before it was a household term

love in the age of quarantine

self-isolation:

- 1- to be ordered by the government to confine yourself to your home for fourteen days to prevent the spread of a virus

- 2- to allow him to drive space between your friends and family
    -to believe you are something toxic to spread
    -to confine yourself to your home for four months

katie feltmate

when you live alone
there is a lot of space to fill
a lot of walls looking back at you
gawking at your loneliness
taunting you to fill these rooms
with new memories
with things that bring you joy
when you live alone
there is a lot of silence
to welcome in thoughts
you haven't allowed in
for years

love in the age of quarantine

i wonder what the neighbors thought
when they heard us screaming
did the vibrations of our voices shake their wine racks
when they heard me yelling that i need to be alone
that you didn't understand the artist in me
when you smashed your phone against the hardwood
i wonder if the elderly woman living below us
mistook it for thunder
looked out of her window for lightning
but only saw the clouds
i wonder how many times
i've mistaken abuse
for the weather

katie feltmate

i know how easy it is
to care for a toxic thing
why one would continue
to tend to a garden of thorns
even when they prick blood
and scar your fingertips
after all it is your garden
and you have been tending it for so long
but aren't you tired of wincing in pain
when someone tries to hold your hand

love in the age of quarantine

why would i run away from a building
that isn't burning
what reason is there to leave if
you are not suffocating in smoke
skin burning
so the floors boards are starting to crack
so what
show me a real reason to leave
so the insulation has disintegrated
show me a real kind of cold
i have survived more
uninhabitable places
than this

katie feltmate

something volatile and frightening
doesn't always stay that way
today he might be a ten-meter wave
and tomorrow he might be the kind of warm water
you want to lay back and immerse your hairline beneath
i know how it easy it is to forget the tsunami
when you give your body
back to the salt
and just
float

love in the age of quarantine

i will not stay
i will not stay
i will not stay
i will not stay
i will not stay
i will not stay
i will not stay
i will not stay
i will not stay
i will not stay
i will not stay
i will not stay
i will not stay
i will not stay
i will not stay
i will not stay
i will not stay
i will not stay
i will not stay
i will not stay
i will not stay
i will not stay
i will not stay
i will not stay
i will not stay
i will not stay
i will not stay
i will not stay
i will not stay
i will not stay
i will not stay
i will not stay
i will not stay
i will not stay
i will not stay
i will not stay

sometimes the people that say they love us
are the ones that hurt us the most

they fall short
like their legs were cut at the knees
like they could never
have loved us properly
from the beginning

"Love" seems to be just another word to most, just something to get what they want and with just one flick love becomes "Hate" it becomes a toxic burning straight through your soul, a word that I feel too deeply since you broke my heart and I only see now that all you were was a toxic man one who couldn't love.

love in the age of quarantine

and if i am to survive this this shipwreck
this new disfigurement of my heart
if i am to get off this vessel
which is holding and sinking me in concurrence
if i am to jump off the portside
into the abyss of blue and swim for land
if i am to tread water without my legs giving out under me
if i am to find dry land to sit and warm myself
if i am to live again
to breathe again
don't ever let me board
a boat like that
again

still
every time i slip my brass key into the lock
i half expect to find you there
sitting on my couch waiting to ambush me
spine erect, eyes trained on the door

still
i slide the chain across the lock
check it four times before i go to bed
heart palpitations synced with every buzzer ring
immense relief when it's just the uber eats delivery
worker and not you lurking in the doorway

still
can't shake the feeling that you have been in my space
sat in my living room for how long
premeditated this or acted on impulse
made a copy of the key how many days
before i kicked you out

still
i don't know what is more violating
unlocking the door to find you there
or the frequency in which the image still
floods my brain

-flashbacks

what was it that you were expecting
that i would be happy to see you
that i would be indifferent to your invasion
that i wouldn't even flinch
perhaps you envisioned
that i would give you another chance
that this breaking and entering
was just a grand romantic gesture
that a crime of passion
isn't really a crime
is this what you thought
this unforgivable breach
would award you

-delusion

katie feltmate

you turned my home into a place of fear
a museum of artifacts of abuse
made my safe space the nucleus of trauma
carved a path for the bad memories you left me with
to set up camp
stained into the wallpaper
clinging to the curtains
living in between the grout in the kitchen tiles
invasive and invisible house pests

before this virus forced us inside
i only stayed here when i had to
spent every waking hour i could
at work or with friends
at the gym, the grocery store
anywhere your shadows
didn't live

but now i am isolated
to the square footage
of wreckage you left for me
forced to work in it
sleep in it
live in it
and there's nowhere else to go

love in the age of quarantine

my friends beg me to change my locks
my therapist says it will bring me comfort
a feeling of safety and control
all i have to do is call my rental company
and tell them what happened
but i can't bring myself to do it
can't pick up the phone
and make the call
can't say it out loud
can't make a statistic
out of myself
today

katie feltmate

a coworker reaches out to tell me
they will support me if i ever need anything
that they've supported *women in my situation*
before and an instinct to downplay it all
like a thick hot bile erupts up my throat
overflowing into
i'm fine
thank you so much
that's so kind of you
but i'm fine
i'm okay

love in the age of quarantine

shame like a common thief
makes ropes and knots of your hands
snatches the words from the tip of your tongue
and shoves them back down the pit of your stomach
leaving with everything but your story
laying on the floor
out of reach

katie feltmate

i'm sorry that i lived with a man
that required us to create a safe word
that it got to the point that you had to ask
if i feared for my safety
if i say *christmas tree*
in a text or on the phone
you know to come running
i'm sorry that that's how
we spent the holidays that year
i'm sorry that this threat is not just insulated
in the hallways of my apartment
but seeping out of the cracks in the sidewalk
i'm sorry that you worry when i walk home
i'm more sorry we live in a world
where something this simple is dangerous
i'm sorry that i feel the need
to apologize for any of this at all

this is the weight of being a woman
carrying the hurt from the threats that surround us
then carrying the pain that it causes those we love

we don't just bear the scars
we spend lifetimes choking
on the second-hand smoke

-to my father

love in the age of quarantine

he chases me down the hallway
spits every obscenity his mother never taught him not to say
christmas tree
i lock the bathroom door and he pounds his fists and kicks
like he is in a sinking car trying to pop the window out
christmas tree
i hear the recession of heavy footsteps
then comes the smashing
the crashing
the breaking
christmas tree
two days later he apologizes
gushing and groveling
i'm sorry, i love you, forgive me

christmas tree
christmas tree
christmas tree

katie feltmate

the mind in love and abuse is dyslexic
words and actions scramble in your brain
you confuse swear words for compliments
crumbs for grand gestures
codependency for love

i don't think that it is a conscious thought
that we deserve abuse or *bad love*
i think it is the absence of a conscious thought
that we only deserve *good love*
maybe it is this lack of intention
that breeds permittance

katie feltmate

all i know is that in the last season of us
i didn't take off my makeup
or wash my face for months
in our sick love, i was so starved
that i bloated my body with all things bad for me
lived off your table scraps and the odd apple core
you would throw down to me
but now, it is my turn
to eat

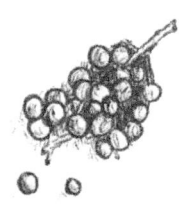

love in the age of quarantine

today i changed my locks
made the call
hired the locksmith
and watched
as he unscrewed my anxiety
and fear from the door
replaced it with a new sense of security
and empowerment
this is my home
and you're not welcome here
.

katie feltmate

i will light incense
i will sanitize every doorknob
light switch and glass
you may have breathed on
i will throw the sheets and pillowcases
into scalding hot soapy water
and do the same with my skin
scrubbing you off of it all
i will drink your beer
and spit it back into the earth
i will reorient my bed so it can have a different view
than the one it had when you last slept here
i will delete your playlist on spotify
sign you out of my netflix
expel you from every corner
of my apartment
every artery of my heart
and call it
spring cleaning
this is *my* home
and i am taking it back

love in the age of quarantine

on day 30 of lockdown
i started making mistakes
unblocked your number
to tend to the guilt tugging at my pant leg
like an overindulged child
we are in a global pandemic after all
how heartless would i be
to deny your pleading
in a time like this
and in one phone call
you morphed from beast to boy
the matted fur of you retracted
into smooth skin follicles
melted down in front of me
staring me straight in the eye
the humanness of you
undeniable

but when i refused to submit to your needs
you became wolf once again
all matted fur and bared teeth
making sounds so sharp
i never imagined your throat
could hold without getting cut
eyes lock-jawed on me
pacing back and forth
nails digging into the wet earth
drool hanging from your jowls
and in this transformation
you became a reminder
that boundaries
are meant to be upheld for a reason
and asserting them
is the bravest act of self-love
i could ever give myself
more powerful
than the snarl
of any beast

love in the age of quarantine

how much emotional labor do we do
for someone who has hurt us
at what point do we wipe the slick
off our brows and sit down
relinquish the halo from our hairline
and submit to our own need for care

katie feltmate

going back to something that hurt you
is a violence to the self

love in the age of quarantine

if i give all of my love and care
to someone who gives nothing back
will i have enough to care for myself
i want to believe love is an infinite resource
that i can endlessly pull it out of my ribcage
like a chain of colorful bandanas from a hat
but what happens if you don't have any magic
left over for yourself

katie feltmate

not everything that is right for you
feels like it in the moment
maybe the first step
is reciting it like a mantra
i can sleep alone
i can live alone
i can be alone
i can face this pandemic
alone

over glasses of chardonnay and charcuterie, a group of girlfriends and i perform a final autopsy on my relationship. dissecting conversations and aggressions between mouthfuls of chocolate and artichoke and asiago dip. a friend who means nothing but well, fails to contain her shock that *out of all the girls she knows*, this happened to me. how was it that *katie*, the fiercely independent feminist wound up in this situation. how was it that *katie* was putting up with this. how is it that *katie* stayed so long in that turmoil. surely, *katie* would be the last person to end up complacent in such treatment. so, i answer her the only way i can. which is to take a deep breath and say that the vines of codependence are tight and unyielding and that no one is immune to the influence and power of abuse and manipulation in an intimate partner relationship. losing yourself is easy when someone is working actively to erode your sense of self. it is a fog-ridden forest you are terrified to leave. but i did. and it is time to retire this shame. i will not carry it any longer. i do not deserve the weight of it. i do not deserve to punish myself for the actions of another. i am letting go and bringing my knees to my chest in embrace. the only thing i deserve is to let the love come back in. to let it wash over me like ointment over one thousand cuts. what i deserve is to be able to stand up straight without the strain of shame curving my spine. now, take my hand and stand up with me, you deserve this too.

katie feltmate

on day 22 of lockdown
my therapist called me
and asked me how i was
and i asked her how she was
and she let out an exhale
like she had been holding
her breath for months

> *-who cares for the mental health of our mental health workers*

love in the age of quarantine

a creeping feeling
of imposter syndrome or doubt
or the aftertaste of rape culture
or something else i can't quite place
like a hair in your mouth you can't retrieve
finds me and steals the pen from my hand
the voice from my throat

who do you think you are to write this
to think that anyone would care
was it really that bad

on some days this voice is enough
to make me put the pen down
retreat from it all
succumb to the belief that i have nothing worth saying
that no one will care or read it or resonate
that i must be remembering things wrong
that i am over dramatizing
that it wasn't that bad
sometimes that voice is so loud and bellowing
i don't write for days, for weeks, sometimes months

and i start believing that i am nobody, nothing
not someone with a story to tell
not a poet, not a survivor, *not both*

katie feltmate

thankfully, there are more days
when i am the straight spine of self-belief
when i drown out that voice and turn the volume
of my own affirmations up higher
this is my life
my experiences
this is my voice
my truth
and it deserves to be heard

and this is what i want you to remember
your experience is valid
your voice is needed
and no one can take that away from you
no one can degrade or dilute it
this narrative belongs to you
your story is yours only
and it matters

love in the age of quarantine

it took me months to learn to sleep alone again
for the separation anxiety to subside
to make less space for the grief
and more room for hope
to love myself again
this had to be learned
practiced
rehearsed
like learning how to ride a bike
or tie my shoes
the codependency
was so ingrained in my body
i felt ill for weeks
couldn't breathe if i was alone
fought off the rise of panic attacks
procreating in my chest every night
needed my mother to stay with me for days
before i could brave this new screaming silence
and then the day came
when i had nothing left
but my own thoughts and feelings
and the only thing i could do
was work through them
the only way out of the fog
was to open my eyes
and move through it
to open my heart
and feel it

katie feltmate

and when there was nowhere else to go
i went inward

excavation

katie feltmate

the mind the body and me
a braid that keeps untangling
a trinity of bickering housemates
tell me how do i escape the noise
when i can't leave my house

when i left for costa rica there was snow on the ground
the world was still moving with an unknowing confidence
kids were still going to school
tucking their boots and gloves into cubbies
with their names written on beige masking tape
people were still rising to the song of their alarm clocks
wiggling into jackets, coffee in hand, heading to the office
planes were still flying and friends were still hugging hello
and my only want was to leave this crime scene behind
go far away, forget, breathe a new air
covid was not yet a word indoctrinated into my vocabulary
three days into the trip and i began to think less about
the reckless driving and sun on my face
and more about borders closing
airlines shutting down
not getting home

katie feltmate

we met
when i stepped off the plane in halifax
and into my vacant apartment
when i turned the key, dropped my bags to the floor
and no one else was around to hear it
when i cooked dinner and set the table for one
when in bed that night it was only my breath to be heard
staccato in the stillness

and here you are
the gravity of you pulling
your presence as prominent as this recycled air
your nature to confine
following me from room to room

you are a guest arrived with three bags
i did not invite
you exist to isolate
your lifespan feels longer everyday
i know you are a necessary ointment
for a sick, sick world
but that doesn't make it any easier

-quarantine

love in the age of quarantine

on day 12 of quarantine
i awoke mourning your lips
reminiscing their indelible ripeness
and all the times i bit into them
without breaking the skin
how you didn't do the same for me
how the sharpest thing about you felt so soft
but maybe
it is not this supposed softness that i miss
but the oneness of committing another body by memory
every freckle an island in the vastness
of your honey brown skin
the thickness of your eyelashes
like reeds i used to watch you water with every blink
the curls of your hair a forest of mixed heritage trees
how easy it is to make foliage out of you
but maybe
i am less botanist and more revisionist
reframing the war in a moment of amnesia
as if i have forgotten how it felt to suffer the explosions
or maybe i am less revisionist and more tireless pathologist
gone back to the lab for the fourth post-mortem
unable to put down the scalpel
and declare the cause of death for what it was
or maybe
i am less gloved hands
and more matted paws
still circling this carcass
still sniffing at the bones

katie feltmate

it is the oddest thing to search for comfort
at the source of the pain

you have worked so hard to create new pathways
don't start reinforcing old ones now

katie feltmate

in this new world i am having trouble breathing
so i write to release the air pressure lodged in my lungs
i write to understand, to discover, to process, to heal
maybe to bleed
i curate my environment, play soft music so it flows
into my living room
engulfing me in introspection
i light a scented candle
sit cross legged on the plush carpet
and i write
in this new world
i thought this was a kindness
that unscrewing the faucet
was a service to myself
but there are some days when the water levels
run too high and i am surrounded
some days when i can't turn the tap back off
can't stop the water from rising
some days when every line i write
feels like the dial turned up a little hotter
then comes the steam
then comes the bubbles
rising from the edges of the room
then comes the flush of my skin
red and medium rare
forehead slick
raisin fingertips
boiled down
to my marrow
tell me
how do i write myself
out of the pot

-boiled alive

love in the age of quarantine

a sickness fell onto the world
armed with speed
designed to slow
all we could do
was climb into our homes
and be still
and it was then
that the earth
took her first breath
of the century

katie feltmate

maybe 2020 was the year of reckoning
maybe this was mother nature's long overdue push-back

love in the age of quarantine

to fear quarantine is to know the pain
in the absence of companionship
is to know the desire for true connection and love
is to be in touch with our most basic human needs

katie feltmate

you were always here
as present in our lives
as the particles we breathe
microscopic
we didn't see you
didn't recognize the scope of your reach
underestimated your might
your ability to cause upheaval
from flat calm to storm surge
you, a dormant volcano perched
on an hourglass waiting
for the last grain of sand to fall
we act like you are showing yourself
to us for the very first time
like you barged into our dining rooms
the uninvited dinner guest
it's been months now
and we are still indignant
at your presence

-uncertainty

love in the age of quarantine

write the book
                                        draft that screenplay
relax and enjoy the solitude
                                             lose that 10 pounds
                               don't use this time to lose weight
stay productive   make a schedule
practice self-care
               watch netflix
start a charity
        save your money
                                 go for walks get exercise
              stay at home don't go outside
                      clean out your house
         rest

                               -noise

katie feltmate

i am lying in bed alone
on what i think is a sunday night
when the realization engulfs me
like the ravishing flames of a kitchen grease fire
that i have no one to ride out this apocalypse with
no arms wrapped around me to double as a dream catcher
no other heart to soothe me in my sleep but my own

love in the age of quarantine

quarantine couples
melt together on the couch
like chocolate over a double boiler
soft and slow
velvet sweet and warm
every day is netflix and chill
every day is *good morning beautiful i'm here for you*
check the news updates together
prepare to hear the case counts together
face it all together
make love three times a day
because there is no shortage of free time
or love to cash in so they
cash it in *together*
make the sharp
a little softer
the night
a little shorter
the love
a little louder

katie feltmate

sometimes i am too tired
to cloak my depression in metaphor
to dress it up and clog its pores with alliteration
sometimes
i just don't want to eat
don't want to get out of bed
don't want to be
here

and there isn't a more artistic way to say it

survival guide for pandemic living

1. only check the news when you must
2. go for a walk outside at least once a day
3. call a friend or family member every night
4. move your body, somehow
5. meditate
6. do something you used to do in your old life

katie feltmate

i have spent many
days
hours
years
of my life
in a lack of awe
that i am alive

and this is my greatest tragedy

my friend calls this phenomenon *depression room*
when the place you are supposed to go to for rest
becomes a landfill of used towels on the floor
half-read books hanging off the bookshelf
earrings not put away
when your carpet becomes a junkyard
of mismatched socks and sweaters
and jeans you were never going to wear anyway
a mound so big a family of mice
could build a two-storey nest in
when your bureau and nightstand become servers' tables
neglected to get bussed, with a trail of ants
stuck in the jam plate
and this is how i knock
at the door of my mind
to ask if everything is alright
and come to find
that it's not

katie feltmate

it's month 5 of the pandemic
and i feel strong and empowered
because i woke up every day
and made my body sweat before i gave it fuel
and my body has gotten stronger but not any bigger
and apparently this is what a successful quarantine looks like
i guess i should be thankful for my fear of peanut butter
and other high calorie foods that i banned for this season
i guess i should praise myself for eating rice cakes
and plain chicken breast
for counting each calorie
for running twice as far if i ate something *bad*
for all of the restricting and measuring and obsessing
after all it brought me here
to this place
of eighteen-hour fasts
where i can't see a piece of bread
and not see a point value or 130
how wonderful it is here
this place where i perform a body check
in every mirror i pass
this place where food has moral value
and negative self-talk flourishes
growing from the watering
of six liters of water
poured into
an empty
stomach

love in the age of quarantine

fat phobia and this virus
lie in constant competition for our mental real estate

it's another night in lockdown / podcast on full volume / the voices make me feel less alone/ it's a night where i wish i smoked weed so i could relax / so i could distract myself from this waiting / but i don't / so all i do is sit and steep / in my feelings / in realty / a friend i met in vienna once said to me / he didn't know how people go through life sober / what day is it / baggy t-shirt on / pajama shorts / hair up / plug the sparkly lights in / light a candle / wishing the days away / trying to fill my time / by supper i've almost made it through / five hours of netflix for dessert / four rice cakes with peanut butter and jam for dessert / guilt and body measurements for dessert / it's almost that time again / to go to bed and hope tomorrow / i wake up happier / that tomorrow will be better / that tomorrow case numbers will be lower / that tomorrow i'll love myself / a little more / tomorrow i'll be more grateful / for this life / tomorrow we will be one day closer / to seeing the people who mean the most to us / again / right now it's me / and the stillness / right now it's just boredom / and depression / and covid fatigue

love in the age of quarantine

we are living through
a global pandemic
and people are dying
but anyone who has the privilege to
is more worried about getting bigger
coming out of quarantine with
a higher body fat percentage
less palatable for mainstream consumption
and i have been victim to this too
i still have days when it is easier
to walk on a carpet of broken glass
than look at myself in the mirror
and this is a sadness
a betrayal to the body
a violence to the self
an epidemic
neatly packaged
into the seams
of this pandemic

you can't run from it
can't turn on your tv
or look at your phone
to get away from it
can't tell it to go away
and watch it walk out the door
it will find you
when you are sitting alone
driving home from work
it will come for you
when you are in a dead sleep
all you can do is breathe
just try to breathe
through it
all we can do is hope
just hope
it won't last

-depression as a global pandemic

love in the age of quarantine

the world has already changed
can you see it
do you choose to believe it yet
can you feel it in the air
this heaviness none of us
knows yet how to carry
the air so much thinner here
in this place unrecognizable
where we grieve for the world
we once knew
for the lives we once lived in utter ignorance
that the liberties we took for granted
ever had an expiry date
we lived in disbelief
that the mundane and monotony
could ever be taken away from us
and that we would actually
mourn for it

katie feltmate

in all of your magnificence
you remain perched triumphantly
collecting dust, unworn, untraveled
my shoes, once a tool, now simply decor
accessories that have become obsolete
over the evolution of two weeks
the black boot heels that carried me
over sidewalks into bars from across the world
the white lace-ups that got stomped on
at many an underground club in berlin
the burgundy heels i used to wear to my office job
thank you for all the places you have taken me
for the cigarette butts, broken glass and sticky floors
you shielded me from
for the mountains i climbed with you
for the outfits you complemented
i hope to be able to wear you all again
next time, with a little more
gratitude

if i could trade
all of this emptiness and uncertainty
for a thousand monday morning meetings and small talk
i would

katie feltmate

i have to believe this was all meant to be
that there is work i am meant to do now
that maybe somehow it is an oddly packaged gift
this time we have now
this lethargic pace
there has never been a better time
to go inward
to go further in ourselves
than we have ever ventured before
to become one with our loneliness
until this solitude feels like freedom

love in the age of quarantine

go inward
until you have learned
every childhood wound
by heart
until you have zipped
yourself inside out
and learned to love
every stitch

katie feltmate

i look at old photos of myself as i was when i was so bold
and so free, like i was some girl i used to know
i wonder how she had the courage to do all that she did
i miss her, i want to take a risk with her
climb a mountain alone again, explore a new city again
learn a new language because you have to, to get around again
she seems like a distant memory now, the glint of her fading
away like watching a silver locket sink into the ocean like a
photo bleached out from its frame being too close to the
window sill, i feel like pieces of me are eroding with the tide
all these years, it's hard to believe she ever existed
that she walked the roads that she did
made the memories that she did
all the while never knowing
there could ever exist a time
when this kind of freedom of the road
could be taken away from her

love in the age of quarantine

i have been grieving you for months
maybe years
i looked for you for so long
in all the corners
i thought you may have hidden
waited for you to come back to me
to show me you were still here
there were times i caught a glimpse of you
in the weak spot of my blinders
and it felt so good to have you back
but you never stayed long
you couldn't have lived here
i felt the absence of you
like an open wound in my abdomen
never quite healing, tearing when i moved
i cried for you on so many tuesday nights
and sunday mornings
mourned you before i realized
it was *you* that was missing
still i waited for you by the window each night
hoping you would find your way back home
but it wasn't until i remembered your name
held it on my tongue and called to you
with intention and a desperate welcoming
that you finally came back to me
i thought i needed to resurrect you
but all this time you were here
waiting for me to let you back in
i spent so much time looking for you in the distance
when you were underneath the soles of my feet
this whole time

-a love letter to my independence

katie feltmate

we can only be at peace
when we are in harmony
with our inner self
we can only move through
what we know
with the understanding
we have right now
we can only try to do
what feels right
what feels like us

i am still trying to figure it all out. how to date again, how to heal, how to stop overeating. how to exercise the way i used to in celebration of my body not punishment. i am still at war with my body most days and yet every morning, i wake to find that it has worked through the night breathing life into me, pulsing and pushing blood through my veins. this body that flushes out toxins, creates energy, heals me, protects me, fights infections and illness, keeps me alive in a global pandemic. this body that holds me in a soft sleep until i am ready for this body to carry me gently back to consciousness. still, i have the audacity to slip my feet off the bed, walk over to the mirror and demand it look different. that its life-giving complex systems are not the most magnificent and beautiful sight to behold in the first place.

katie feltmate

relationships are work
so why should i expect
the one with myself
to be any different

when you are exhausted
when you cannot find meaning
not in the stars
not in the sky
when you are too tired to run
too tired to even walk
when all you can do is crawl
remember you are still
on your way

katie feltmate

discovering more of who you are
is a gift we are given
every day

love in the age of quarantine

on day 42 of lockdown
i marched into the bathroom
and looked into the mirror
at a pillar of beauty and strength and resilience
i was ignorant to for so many years
and i told her that i loved her
and i reminded her of all that she has overcome
and i chanted a mantra of permission
feel these feelings and feel them fully
let them come in
leave yourself so open
        that they float in as easily
                as they evaporate
                      out

        of
                      you
there is power in this osmosis
there is healing in this exchange
feel this feeling and write the poetry
until you have worked this feeling out of your skin
like needle and splinter
all prick and blood and reprieve
you know now how to do this
how to visit graveyards
and come back feeling more alive
how to tend an open wound
without contracting infection
how to go into a dark place
and come out illuminated

katie feltmate

when you catch yourself holding
your breath in a white-knuckled grip
notice how the rest of your body
is held too in this duress
how this anxiety metastasizes
through your veins
from root to crown
like a thick invasive sap
lay on your back
let the petals of your tired eyes close
place a hand over your ribs
and breathe
let your lungs find their fullest form
their greatest expression
and breathe deeply
purposefully and know
that each breath you take
is a warning bell switched off
the relief your body is begging for
a love song to the self

-sing

love in the age of quarantine

you don't have to call it quarantine
if that scares you
if it makes you feel caged or confined
call it an act of courage for the earth
call it photosynthesis in reversal
us giving the *trees* the air to breathe
call it a necessary stillness
after centuries of unchecked movement
call it a gift you have within you to give
call it a lesson that must be learned
call it the greatest act of love
we could ever
give to each other

katie feltmate

2020 has been the heaviest year of my life
a weighted blanket of anxiety, uncertainty, and heartache
there was hopelessness and fear
but there was also rejuvenation and regrowth
my life is no longer as infinite as it once felt
now there is only before covid and after covid
two worlds in opposition to each other
struggling to merge into one new reality
and in this new world
i think i am ready
to get back up

love in the age of quarantine

there is the fear of being alone
the trepidation of a lifestyle change
like new skin you don't know how it will fit
there is the anxiety of learning to sleep alone again
the loneliness of a four-person table set for one
the grief of living in a museum filled
with artifacts of old loves past

but greater than fear and grief
is the hope
of solace in solitude
rejuvenation in reduction

greater than fear and grief
is the freedom
of an unbridled mind
a regenerated heart, a healing body

greater than fear and grief
is the faith
of new muscle memory forming
an orchestra of synapses exploding into fireworks

katie feltmate

i wonder when all this is over
if holding hands
will feel as intimate
as a kiss

holding hands

love in the age of quarantine

when we finally rise
from the confinement
of this quarantine
when social distancing
becomes a concept
we are trying to forget
when staying away from people
is an instinct we are trying to unlearn
when we are once again allowed to hold
the same 6 feet of space together
when human touch is no longer a catalyst
for a rippling effect of sickness and death
i want the first hands to hold mine
to be yours
i want your lips to be the first
to graze mine without this trepidation
i want you to be the one to teach me
how to remember this kind of touch
i want your hands to be the river
running down my body
that breaks this endless
drought

katie feltmate

how now do we show this kind of love
the kind of love that is slow and gentle
that warms not engulfs, comes alive in moments
of playful laughs and eye contact
grows from the music of *how are you* sung sweetly
it is a delicate process on a good day
how now do we court in quarantine
when you can't see the pink pomegranates of my cheeks
ripen at the mention of your name
when you can't hear the bat of my eyelashes
from across the phone line
there is not a lot of space for grand gestures now
or the non-verbal communication we've been relying on
maybe now
this type of love requires more honesty
less scribbling of hidden meanings
to be decoded between long glances
and surface conversation
maybe now
this kind of love requires more intention
must be deliberate to stay alive
or maybe now
this kind of love is meant to be patient
to allow distance to have its hour
until it becomes time once again
for *this kind*
of love

love in the age of quarantine

if i could
i'd make the sun shine
on your back deck every day
i'd make sure the grocery store
was never crowded when you go
that your favorite coffee was always on sale
that lysol wipes were never out of stock
i would send you peace and contentment
in the mail every week
so you always had something to look forward to
i'd intercept your grocery delivery
and write love poems
on the inside of your cereal boxes

katie feltmate

hey, i don't know what the world is going to look like two weeks from now but i am wondering if you would be interested in joining me for a glass of wine on video call. i'll brush my eyelashes black and paint my lips hibiscus and spray vanilla perfume on my collar bones as if you could smell it. and we can hold on to these holograms of each other tighter than all of the moments we took for granted like a month ago, when the real you and the real me sat on my couch sipping port and there was no lag when i batted my eyelashes at you and you lobbed a smile back and you *could* see the red of the wine staining the edge of my mouth merging into my lipstick like a tiny coral sunset and you *could* smell the vanilla perfume off my collar bones when i leaned over you to top up your glass. that night i wanted you to touch me. and all that stood in our way was your chivalry and the delicate jurisdiction of new love territory. tonight, i still want you to touch me. and all that stands in our way is government orders a state of emergency and one- thousand-dollar fines. so i'll settle for computer screens and texting if i have to. but i guess what i'm saying is i want to know the blue of your eyes again. want to hear the fullness of your laugh not warped through desktop speakers. want to watch the flush ripple through your cheeks like a drop of red food coloring into a glass of milk when i say something unexpectedly forward and you clear your throat and comb back your hair. i don't care if we have to be six feet apart. two meters is nothing compared to the distance that separates us
now the days laid out like
a never-ending highway
stretched out
before us for
miles

-unsent texts

love in the age of quarantine

to be lonely is to be starved
of the food that sustains us
the energy that moves us
the connection that nurtures us
the love that heals us

katie feltmate

when the world finally opened back up
like a break in the clouds after 1000 days of rain
we were so eager to step out into the sunlight
and into the warm cocoon
of new love

love in the age of quarantine

we fell in love in an age of scarcity
in a world of panic and hoarding and fear
i walked away from the storm
to the flat calm of your coastline
of course i wanted to lay there
in this island we created
we were two people
who had been treading water so long
of course we wanted to live there
of course this dry land
felt like
eden

katie feltmate

we can feel it
this unsteadiness, this earthquake
the ground underneath our feet forever shifted
the earth's tectonic plates once again out of place
the whole world hanging
a little crooked

love in the age of quarantine

what is loneliness
if not the unrelentless ache of withdrawal
from the one drug we cannot live without
were not meant to live without
it is the sweating, skin crawling, splitting headache
the craving, deafening, sleepless existence
the constant alerts ringing in unison
from the cathedral of your body, mind and heart
echoing down every chamber in your body
something is missing
something is missing
something is missing
something is missing
something is missing
something is missing
something is missing

katie feltmate

does it nourish you
when you breathe it in
and allow it space
does it make you feel
like coming home to yourself
do you listen to it
the voice swelling
like a wave inside of you
do you honour it
the tiny compass of a heart
charting a path only for your feet
do you take it
the hand of your authentic self
reaching out to you
do you hold space for it
the deepest truths and
longings buried below
do you move through it
in harmony with what is
do you listen to it

love in the age of quarantine

why do i feel like leaning on him
will skew my sense of balance
like independence is a product of muscle memory
and if i stop flexing i'm going to lose it
what about all the times that muscle meant survival
when it meant being able to pull myself
up over the ledge
how do i know
i won't be down there
again

katie feltmate

just as quickly as new love can blossom
so too can it begin to fade

love in the age of quarantine

they say a bouquet of roses
takes three weeks to fully wilt and decay
three weeks for their heads to bow lower and lower
until they break off
it took us six months to begin wilting
six months for you to no longer revel in the newness of me
or hold me like it was a privilege to be in my space
six months for you to no longer hear music in my breathing
you used to feel electrified laying in bed with me
couldn't believe how close you had gotten
but just like all new and sparkly things we bring home
eventually they start to blend in
with the coffee machine and decor
just something you picked up once
and have now

katie feltmate

that weekend away
i needed you to touch me
to remind me that we are in love
and everything is okay
i needed to feel close to you somehow
to know that what was can still be
that we are not just two regular people
who have lost their spark so early on
that there is still heat here enough
to keep us warm through this winter
but when i looked
out of the window
all i saw was frost

love in the age of quarantine

one sunday morning we sat in the sun on the couch
and i read you a poem i had just written through tears
a poem i had written to shapeshift
trauma into healing
frailty into strength
the stitching of an open cavern, shut
you looked at me and said
you write about him so much even i'm starting to miss him
and that is the moment
you began losing me

katie feltmate

i can't be with someone
who doesn't see me ~~clearly~~

of course this dry land *felt* like eden
it was a soft place to land
after i had known
such sharpness

you were the kinder love
the gentler love
the love that came after the wreckage
that came after the loudness
i fell out of that burning building
jumped from that ship
and swam for the shore
and you met me *there*
soaking wet and shivering
still coughing up smoke
you scooped me up into your arms
brushed off the ash and dried my clothes
enveloped me in a warmth
i hadn't felt for so long
i hardly recognized it
you were supposed to be the safer love
the better love
the love that made all
the burns on my arms
the water in my lungs
worth it
i thought you were my safehouse
a place where i could finally breathe
but how could i have really known
what a home should feel like then
hair still reeking of smoke
seasick and starving

your emotional brain and logical brain
don't know each other, they've never met
they don't speak the same language
don't realize that they live in the same building
your emotional brain is the footsteps stomping
in the ceiling at 4 in the morning
the noise your logical brain doesn't understand
but is constantly interrupted by

-conversations about heartache with my brother

katie feltmate

safe love feels like solid ground
like a straight line
like predictability
like the absence of anxious thoughts
and panic at the drop of a pin
like hair not parachuting off of your scalp
because you're stressed and not eating
safe love feels like saying, *this is how i am feeling*
with no fear of retaliation or punishment
safe love feels like no second guessing
no guessing at all, just assurance, peace
permission to make mistakes
and to learn from them
safe love feels like i know you'll answer if i call
like i know you won't leave when i need you
like there's no part of me you don't accept and embrace
i can only speak of what safe love feels like
by thinking about
what i know
it does not

love in the age of quarantine

the thing about humans
is that we can change our minds
our hearts
our desires
and that's a hard truth
if you are the one being left behind

katie feltmate

how dare i take my love back
after i spent christmas with your family
after we saw sunsets and mountains together
after you framed a photo of us
after i wrote you love poems
after we indulged in visions of a life shared
how dare i take that love back
and pour it into myself

it is hard knowing
that i am the villain in your story
i'm sorry that i spotted our incompatibility first
that what were mountains to me
were only molehills to you

-two realities

katie feltmate

it was not just the heartache
but the accompanying guilt
that consumed me

i am tired of healing
tired of rehearsing this routine
like it is an act i will perform
in front of a crowd someday
tired of pulling my limp body from the ground
and rebuilding each vertebra in my spine
back up until i can stand again
i am tired of self-soothing
of affirming myself
i am not tired of acquiring the tools
but of having reasons
to use them

katie feltmate

your inner voice
does not promise you
that honoring it won't hurt
it does not promise you
the easiest path to walk
it is not here to protect you
from the pain of difficult choices
it is here to help you make them
to guide you towards what you truly desire
so you can architect the authentic life
that you deserve
so that you can be
have and achieve
everything you were put on this earth to do

love in the age of quarantine

i just want to be on the other side of heartbreak

katie feltmate

we don't just say goodbye to our partners
but to their parents
their siblings
their friends
the family dog
all of the ancillary relationships
we no longer have access to
we grieve
in concurrence

love in the age of quarantine

it happens gradually
the unraveling
today you change your lock screen
tomorrow you take down the photos in your room
on thursday you take off his ring
on saturday you have a girl's night so you can laugh again
on sunday you go into nature
on monday when it all starts again you call your friend allison
and journal every time you get the urge to text him
this unwiring
this weaning off
doesn't happen overnight

katie feltmate

you can love
and let go
at the same time

love in the age of quarantine

comfort and support
does not have to come
from a romantic relationship

katie feltmate

why should my allegiance be to anyone but my inner voice
who else should i consider taking guidance from

love in the age of quarantine

they won't be coals or forest fire
they will be the gentle crack of a fireplace
they won't be a jealous ocean
the right one is a current
strong enough to carry you
when you are tired
but gentle enough
to bring you back home

-the right one

katie feltmate

you realize now
you only deserve to be touched by soft things

linking arms

love in the age of quarantine

there is no way you can be alone in quarantine
when the entire world is sitting beside you
counting down the days just the same
scrolling on instagram on the other side of the wall
across the street from your house
in the countries rubbing shoulders
with you across the sea
i know if i look outside my window
i will meet the gaze of a million eyes
all watching to see what unfolds
i know if i press my ear up against the glass
will hear a symphony of instruments
being plucked on rooftops
across the world

katie feltmate

maybe this swelling of our lungs
is not a death sentence but a message
maybe it's not meant to close our eyes
but to pry them open
like a car accident you can't look away from
like wreckage you can't help but draw meaning from
maybe this newfound slowness was to caution us
that the earth can only take so much
destruction and rebuilding
before her legs give out
underneath us all

love in the age of quarantine

i
wonder
how mother
nature feels about
us crafting metaphors
around her. drawing greedily
from the spring of her for inspiration.
do her cheeks flush with the colours of
the sunset when we mention her, or does
she bow her head into wet moss defeated as she
watches us take and take and take but never grasp.
us poets, continually churning metaphors out of her
complexity. spinning gold from grass, blue from sky but doing
nothing to preserve it. i wonder what the poets of the future
will have
to write
about in
50 years

-to be a poet is to be an environmentalist

katie feltmate

this pandemic will sit
indelible in our minds
like tattoos on our psyche
like history we will tell
our grandchildren about

what is a global pandemic
if not a microscope on privilege

katie feltmate

you are sitting in the comfort of your home
unnerved by the emptiness that you see on the streets
your body reacting to this foreign silence like it is a violence
remember there are people sitting in their homes
who are forced to listen to the soundtrack of planes overhead
of bombs and screaming and explosions
whose air is filled with smoke and blood and panic
the silence you exist in here
is a sign of peace
is a sign of unity
is a sign of sacrifice and love
of a collective action
don't take this for granted

love in the age of quarantine

i once saw a women at costco buy fifteen packages
of lysol wipes and two carts full of toilet paper
another day i saw a man try to buy out the entire row
of thermometers at the pharmacy
which was at least 10
until the clerk told him
only one per customer
then one day i saw a man
giving out food from the back of his van
to folks whose assistance cheques hadn't come in yet

-the hoarder and the helper

katie feltmate

is there a word in the english language
for the feeling of losing someone
not to the most significant threat facing the world at the time
but to something so seemingly random and unrelated
something needless and inexplicable

there is a small town in rural nova scotia called portapique
it has about 100 year-round residents
it is a bucolic paradise of rolling hills
it is a place where neighbors know each other
and what their kids do for a living
it's cottage country in the summer
a place where families gather around the tv
watch the news at six and remark
on the terrible things that happen in big cities
but never experience them firsthand
it is a place of peace and retirement and farming
and on april 18-19 it was a place where a man
impersonated a police officer and committed
the deadliest mass shooting in canadian history

katie feltmate

we cannot hold you with our hands
and for this we grieve harder
for this the air hangs thicker
in a world that was already so difficult to breathe through

how do you begin to heal in a time
when not even the solace of ceremony is permitted
when the empty stomachs of churches and community halls
starved of patrons lay helpless
their mouths stitched shut
ribs collecting dust like old skin

we are learning how to love differently now
leave the casserole dish on the doorstep
light a candle by the window
chalk a message in the sidewalk

we cannot hold you with our hands
so we will hold you from afar
tenderly like a newborn baby
birthed into this loss
crying and covered in the stickiness of grief
forced out into the aftermath of trauma
we are here waiting on the other side to catch you
to envelope you in our thoughts
swaddle you in the soft blanket of our prayers

close your eyes and listen
to the rhythm of 940,000 hearts beating just for you
a symphony of drums, our collective grief a bass line
love, the song on all of our lips

-for portapique and the families

love in the age of quarantine

we remember you, we love you

heidi stevenson
lisa mccully
sean mcleod
alanna jenkins
emily tuck
jolene oliver
aaron tuck
jamie and greg blair
corrie ellison
gina goulet
tom bagley
kristen beaton
joey webber
john joseph zahl
elizabeth joanne thomas
lillian campbell hyslop
dawn madsen
frank gulenchyn
heather o'brien
joy and peter bond

katie feltmate

this pain is going to linger
longer than the lifetime of these headlines
longer than the virtual vigil
and the letters arriving at your door
longer than the wilt of the flowers
laid on the roadside memorial
but i want you to know
we have not forgotten
we will not forget
we see you
we love you
we are your
community

love in the age of quarantine

if you have lost someone you love
i won't implore you to heal
to patch up this loss like it is a gash
and not the gaping hole of a cannon ball
burst through your chest
a concentric circle, cut out like dough
still raw and smoking
i won't tell you to package it up pretty
with something silver and shiny and easier to swallow
won't tell you to sew a lining around this tear
to make out of it something finished
or repaired

katie feltmate

grief has no drying time
only a
dampening

love in the age of quarantine

right now, she sits
on the pink floral of her new couch by the windowsill
drowning in a viscous silence
dead air punctuated by the ticking clock in the bedroom
it's face drooped over prairie-flat sheets
she still walks into the den expecting to find him in his chair
still reaches for his pillbox to organize his week
still looks out the window at the chickadees and wishes
he could watch them dance the way he used to
with wonder and the love he had
for all god's creatures
is there a word for this type of loneliness
for the sorrow of living alone in a global pandemic
in the same home you shared
with your partner of over 60 years
how do you describe with justice
this brand of isolation

this type of breaking

the thickness of this bleeding
how do you sleep in such a restless place
in air so steeped with memories
the ghost of lifetime love ever-present
in the absence of his slippers by the bed
still the corners of her mouth
find purpose to lift
laughter still reverberates from her chest
her hands, soft and worn from holding
so many grandchildren
still rest with unwavering resolve
over the gold cross that has adorned her neck
since birth

katie feltmate

when everything else in this life
is a fluid river of change
when the future of our world
is the shake of pointed toes on a balance beam
my grandmother's faith
is the ground that remains unmoving

and i think this believing
might just be
how you survive
it all

how do you describe this compounding effect of pain
grief layered upon other grief
like the walls of an apartment
in an 80-year-old building
repainted coat after coat after coat
like a russian doll
crack our wooden bodies in half to discover
pain
    within
        pain
            within
                pain

katie feltmate

what must it feel like
to be given a stage four cancer diagnosis
in the throes of a global pandemic
is it the whoosh of all of the oxygen in the room sucked out
is it the pelting of rain in an already dark sky
is it the ringing of a house full of smoke alarms
you can't turn off and no one else can hear
is it a punchline that missed its audience
is it the kind of news you once thought was reserved
for beds on wheels and skin more worn than yours
not for a 26-year-old standing at the precipice of life
i remember that night in my apartment when you felt that
small golf ball in your neck, how you were halfway to
america for treatment when the announcement came that the
borders were closing, i remember when your fridays turned
into chemo and your weekends blurred into nausea, when it
became too dangerous for you to get on public transit, i
remember the long shifts destiny had to endure to be there
for your appointments and all the while you found a way to
joke, to keep alive your sense of humor, i remember your
boundless resiliency, how you took it all on at once, a global
pandemic, a cancer diagnosis, how you had to put off life for
a while and here you are now, cancer free
and after all that i can't imagine an obstacle
you couldn't overcome
and after all our world lost this year
i am forever grateful we didn't lose you

-for emory

our life plans stand face to face with uncertainty
and lose every time

katie feltmate

i think about how often we go to that place
that is so dark and cold and soaked in despair
how our minds seem to drift downstream so quickly
how we pick up potential trauma
in the storage closets in our minds
how we dress it up give it a name
keep it as a house pet
feed it our energy and thoughts
how we catastrophize and extrapolate
until it's all so vivid so real we can taste it
the blood, the infidelity, the deceit, the grief
the metallic flavor of our manufactured fears
but if we can so easily slip down into this place
and cause ourselves to feel so intensely
then can't we teach ourselves to glide intentionally
into a place of joy and self-love and fulfillment
maybe this means moving upstream
maybe this is a practice
maybe someday
we can live there
instead

-meditate

there is power in acknowledging our emotions
naming them like types of weather
we are simply experiencing
you can choose
to be terrified of the liquid falling from the sky
trickling down your windowpane
or you can call it *rain*
you can try to hide
from the force howling against your house
shaking the trees and stirring the leaves outside
or you can call it *wind*
you can call it temporary
just a weather system
passing through

katie feltmate

it is easy on blue sky days
to step outside and feel what you feel
when you feel good
to absorb the sun on your face
but when is the last time you stepped outside
with the purpose of feeling the rain
let it truly permeate your skin
leaned in to the wet and the chill
and called it for what it was
for what it is

love in the age of quarantine

on may 25, 2020
they snuffed out your dignity
like pressing the lid on a candle
pushing the hard rubber of their
white supremacy on your neck
flattening your body into the pavement
they heard your pain and did nothing
heard your gasps for air and did nothing
your pleading
your desperation
your calls to your mother
and nothing
this plague has been mutating long before
covid-19 was a household term

-for george floyd

katie feltmate

we gathered in numbers now illegal
in a closeness that had become forbidden
armed with hand sanitizer and grief
we shouted and cried and chanted
kneeled in a sea of protest
risked community spread
because the stakes were too high
to stay inside

love in the age of quarantine

pandemic or not
we had no choice
but to march to the streets
and challenge a plague
that has lived much longer than this virus
and in my city
it was regarded as the most white support
the blm movement had seen
which is not a congratulation
but a shameful realization
that it took this long
for the white community to show up
to understand our responsibility
to bring these systems down
it took time
it took time
but we are here now
standing as a collective
voices echoing
even with our mouths masked
by a thousand different coloured cloths
if all we can see now
are each other's eyes
at least now
they are
open

katie feltmate

we are starting to wake from it now
beginning to shed these thick layers
we have been wearing all quarantine
the ice is starting to melt
we are unthawing as a nation
as a world
as a species
and we will start
moving again soon
just as fast as we have before
will this resurrection
be our downfall
or our most courageous act

a vaccine has been developed in record time
and it is said to be the fastest approval of a vaccine
meant for global distribution our world has ever seen
not because the clinical trials were rushed
not because the vaccine hasn't been tested enough
but because *the entire world came together to do this*
countries and governments and millionaires
funded and prioritized this research over all else
we had the will and resources of the world behind this
and we did it
just imagine
what else we could accomplish
if we work together

katie feltmate

we were all impacted by this storm
some countries more than others
some families more than others
some demographics more than others
we were all touched by covid-19
and doesn't that reinforce
how much we need to take care
of each other

-what else are we here for

love in the age of quarantine

who could be better equipped
to deal with this crisis, than the artists
we already have the tools to take hurt
and turn it into art
stick our fingers in our cuts
and spin paint from blood
splash it on a canvas
reach into our toolkits
chisel away at the trauma laden in the clay
and find metaphor, reason, truth, love
we've been doing this our whole lives
this may just be the greatest project of all
the inspiration we never asked for

katie feltmate

a child adapts to wearing a mask
the same way they adapt to learning to use a spoon
without question, without any baseline of comparison
but don't forget about the teenagers
who have had the joys of youthhood
their juvenescent rites of passage
stolen from them
there will be no walking across the stage
to the sound of cheers this year
no glancing into the auditorium
to catch the eye of a pair of proud parents
and grandparents beaming
there will be no prom night
or afterparty hangover
no freshmen week parties
or in-classroom learning
just screens
and slideshows
and separation

love in the age of quarantine

my brother's partner shayna
was born with an oversized heart and kind eyes
she takes care of older folks whose memories
have left them without notice
she brings softness into their homes
she is a calming presence
she is a reassuring voice
some days she is a granddaughter
other days she is nameless
but she is always structure and routine
pills organized on the counter
dinner warmed up on the table
someone to eat with
she is laughter in a lonely place
warmth in a cold room
companionship

> then the pandemic hit
> and she had to start wearing masks to their
> homesand it was then that she became
> *stranger*
> became sickness and uncertainty
> became something faceless and
> unfamiliarbecame danger
> became heartbroken
> for the trust she had lost

one afternoon one of her clients a man in his 80's
asks her for just one last favor before she leaves
please, can you take off your mask so i can see you
she tells him to look through his living room window
unlatches the front door and walks outside
stands up to the glass and pulls the thin cloth off
looking down at her, his face blossoms into a smile
oh you have dimples my dear
your smile
you look so
human

love in the age of quarantine

just because the pandemic is easing
just because we are slowly inoculating our sick world
with the pointed tip of a needle
does not make the pain and suffering
of these years disappear for everyone
for some, this pandemic was an inconvenience
like sitting in traffic or waiting in a long line for coffee
but for others, this pandemic will not be so easy
to walk away from
for others this pandemic has cost them a loved one or many
for others this pandemic has cost them a business, a livelihood
for others this pandemic meant pain that will never fully heal
for others the vaccine may never come
remember this
we did not all experience this pandemic equally
nor will we move forward from it on equal footing

katie feltmate

to the anti-vaxxers
to the covid-19 deniers
to the down-players
i don't care about your platitude that the flu
kills more people than covid-19 every year
all lives have value
every single person on this planet matters
their life mattered and their death matters
every single person lost in this pandemic
is a tragedy to somebody
just because you have not been touched personally
by the pandemic yet
does not erase the impact
to be in a country with triple its population
in vaccines and refuse it
is to be bathed in privilege and waste it
i don't want to hear your statistics about the common cold
when there are countries whose streets are filled with bodies
when there is a world full of lungs heaving through ventilators
when there are millions of people praying
for access to just one dose
when you say you aren't worried about covid
because you're *young and healthy*
all i hear is disregard for your community
to be naive is one thing
to actively work against your global community
is another
this is about more
than you

love in the age of quarantine

i think about the birthday parties that your aunt will miss
the candles she will never blow out
the baby shower that your brother won't be at
the niece he will never hold
the chair at the head of the table
that your father will never tell jokes from again
the grandchildren he will never bounce on his lap
i think about the memories that can't be made now
the moments that will be missed
the possibilities that have evaporated out of reach
for so many families around the world

katie feltmate

to be pregnant in a pandemic
is to be uncertain of the world this child will be brought into
is to wonder if the father will be allowed in the delivery room
is to hold your breath during every update in case numbers is
to grieve the large baby shower you always envisioned
is sharing the sex of the baby over a zoom call
is to do it all in an unprecedented time in history
is to revel in the resilience this tiny growing thing already has
daring to enter the world in such a time
because they just couldn't wait any longer
to meet you

love in the age of quarantine

all any of us really wants
is to feel safe
seen
and loved

    -community

katie feltmate

it's 9:05 p.m. on tuesday may 19
the year is 2020
and i love you already
gas is 79 cents a liter
and i haven't filled up my decade old
hunk of junk i call a car in a month
i'm 24 and i'm eating a bowl of white cheddar
organic mac and cheese
the kind of quick lunch i'll make for you on days
when i am too tired to throw together a veggie platter
with freshly churned hummus, cherry tomato eyes
and a carrot stick mouth
i don't know if i've met your father yet
i don't think i have but sometimes life surprises you
this is just one of the lessons you will learn
this world i am living in today is not the one i was born into
nor will it be the one you will meet headfirst
i hope you never have to experience a pandemic
that by the time you come along
we would have figured out how to be better
how to live with more love and care
for the ground beneath our feet
i am sitting in my apartment in the city
looking outside the window at the lights
and the navy-blue expanse of a sky
that will one day have the privilege
of being reflected in your eyes
and all i can do is hope
we get it right before
you arrive

- time capsule to my future child

love in the age of quarantine

through the chaos and uncertainty
panic and hardship
loss and regrowth
we found love
in messages of hope carved into the sidewalk
in zoom calls with friends and loved ones
in hand-painted signs taped to windowsills
in virtual vigils and online messages
in check-in texts and socially distanced walks
in the sacrifice of a world
moving in slow motion

katie feltmate

love is like a game of i-spy
if you know to look for it
you will notice it
everywhere

an earthquake cracks open japan
and the pressure shatters a glacier in antarctica
do you still think we are not all intrinsically connected

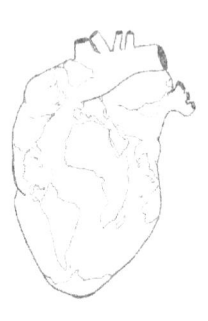

katie feltmate

i fell in love three different times during the pandemic
twice with other people
and finally with myself
and it was the third love
that meant the most
it was the third love
that breathed air back into my lungs
that gave me the courage to walk away
from the bad love
the sick love
the unsafe love
the mismatched love
i fell into the arms of *my own* love
learned how to hold *myself* gently
how to sing *myself* to sleep
how to find comfort in *my own* presence
how to tease gratitude out of each strand of hair on my head
i looked around my home with a new reverence
for the earthquakes it withstood
and the beauty and strength that remained unmoved
and thanked god that i was able to find
this love
in the age
of quarantine

love in the age of quarantine

i have felt deep joy
and i have felt deep pain
both have served me

katie feltmate

there is no sunrise
more magnificent
than the one that took its time to glow
the one that dawns after the longest night
that rises up breaking the cold, the fog, the darkness
to warm itself with its own incandescence

Acknowledgements

I would like to thank all of my loved ones who helped me comb through the debris of a difficult year. Thank you to all of the poets whose work I have consumed, subsisted off and been inspired by, to write this book. Thank you to you, dear reader for coming on this journey with me. Thank you to all of the advocates who have been doing work to make these issues safer and more acceptable to speak about now. Thank you to the BLM advocates for your continued labour in galvanizing this movement and educating privileged people like me. Thank you to Dr. Strang, my local government and country's leadership for putting Covid-19 measures in place to keep us safe. Thank you to all of the front-line healthcare workers globally, who carried the weight of this pandemic on their backs. Thank you to every community, country and individual who put the needs of others ahead of their own and *chose love* in this age of quarantine.

-K

Katie Feltmate currently lives in Halifax, Nova Scotia and plans to publish more books of poetry in the future. Katie is available for book readings, facilitating custom poetry workshops as well as one-on-one writing sessions.

To book an interview or service, please email Katie at connect@katiefeltmate.com with your request.

Socials!

Follow Katie's work on Instagram and Facebook
Instagram/**@oceanshoresandmetaphors**
Facebook/**@oceanshoresandmetaphors**
Email: connect@katiefeltmate.com
Website: KatieFeltmate.com

Resources

Provincial Mental Health Crisis Line: 902-429-8167
Kids Help Phone 1-800-668-6868 or text CONNECT to 686868
https://www.mentalhealthns.ca/find-support
https://www.nsdomesticviolence.ca/get-help
https://women.novascotia.ca/resource-map
https://alicehouse.ca/
https://blacklivesmatter.com/

Printed in Great Britain
by Amazon